In a l

"Will you play ball
with me?" said Maggie.
"In a minute, Maggie,"
said Dad.

2

"I have to rake the leaves."

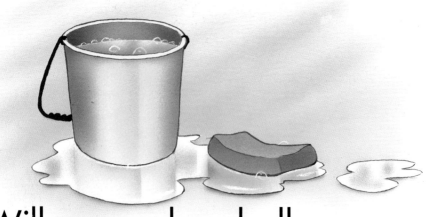

"Will you play ball
with me?" said Maggie.
"In a minute, Maggie,"
said Mom.

7

"I have to wash the car."

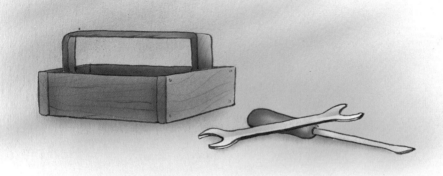

"Will you play ball
with me?" said Maggie.
"In a minute, Maggie,"
said Tom.

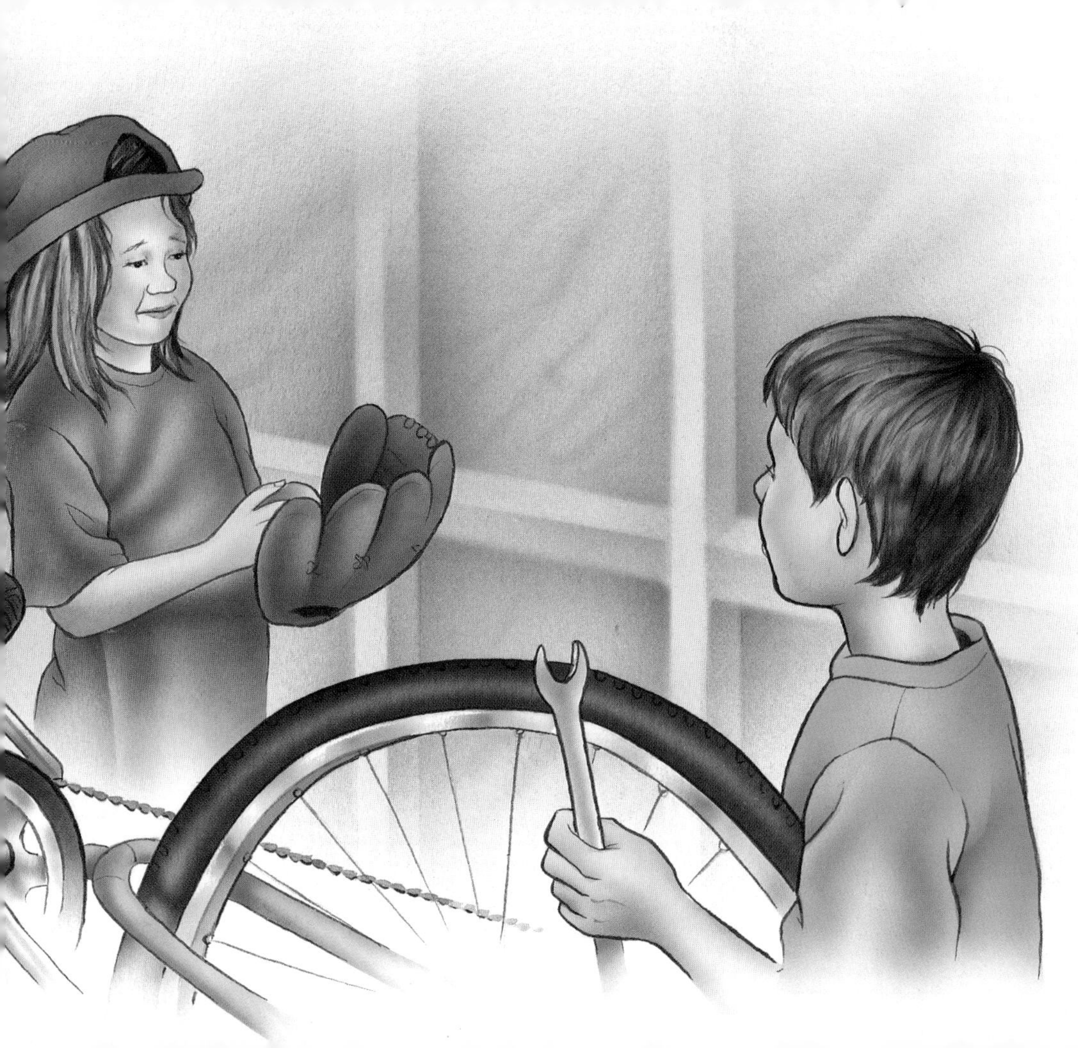

"I have to fix my bike."

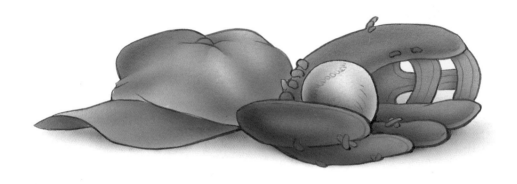

"Maggie, Maggie,"
said Mom and Dad.
"We can play ball, now."

"Zzzz," said Maggie.